Body Needs

WATER and FIBER

for a healthy body

Heinemann Library
Chicago, Illinois

Angela Royston

Created by the publishing team at Heinemann Library
Designed by Ron Kamen and Celia Floyd
Illustrations by Geoff Ward
Originated by Ambassador Litho
Printed in China by Wing King Tong

07 06 05 04 03
10 9 8 7 6 5 4 3 2 1

Library of Congress Cataloging-in-Publication Data
Royston, Angela.
   Water and fiber for a healthy body / Angela Royston.
      p. cm. -- (Body needs)
   Summary: Discusses what water and fiber are, what foods they can be found in, and how the body absorbs, digests and uses these ingredients.
   Includes bibliographical references and index.
   ISBN 1-40340-760-6 (Library bdg. : hardcover)
ISBN 1-40343-314-3 (pbk. bdg.)
   1. Water in the body--Juvenile literature. 2. Fiber in human nutrition--Juvenile literature.   [1. Water in the body. 2. Fiber in human nutrition. 3. Nutrition.]
I. Title. II. Series.
   QP535.H1R695 2003
   612.3'923--dc21

2002012684

Acknowledgments
The author and publishers are grateful to the following for permission to reproduce copyright material: pp. 5, 6, 7, 12, 34, 40, 41 Gareth Boden; pp. 8, 15, 22, 27, 28 (Sygma/Jean Pierre), 30, 33 Corbis; pp. 9, 14, 32, 39, 42 Liz Eddison; pp. 10, 24 Trevor Clifford; pp. 18 (Eye of Science), 19 (Biophoto Associates), 29 (Annabelle Bluesky), 31, 35 (CNRI) SPL; p. 38 Photodisc.

Cover photograph of water and bran flakes, reproduced with permission of Gareth Boden.

Every effort has been made to contact copyright holders of any material reproduced in this book. Any omissions will be rectified in subsequent printings if notice is given to the publisher.

Some words are shown in bold, **like this.** You can find out what they mean by looking in the glossary.

Contents

Why Do We Need to Eat? 4

Water and Fiber 6

What Is Water? 8

Water in Food 10

What Is Fiber? 12

Fiber in Food 14

What Happens in the Digestive System? 16

Water, Fiber, and Digestion 18

Using Fiber 20

Water in the Body 22

Water Balance 24

Water in the Kidneys 26

Too Little Water 28

Too Much Water 30

Too Little Fiber 32

Too Much Fiber 34

Healthy Eating 36

Healthy Drinking 38

Healthy Diets 40

Daily Needs 42

Glossary 44

Further Reading 47

Index 48

Why Do We Need to Eat?

You need to eat and drink to stay alive. All of the food you eat contains **nutrients,** which your body uses to get **energy,** to grow new **cells,** and to get the substances it needs to work properly. If your body lacks nutrients, you will become ill.

Nutrients

Nutrients are divided into groups, according to what they supply. **Carbohydrates** and **fats** supply energy. **Proteins** supply **amino acids**— the building blocks needed to make new cells and repair old cells. **Vitamins** and **minerals** supply chemicals that the cells need in order to work properly. Most foods contain a mixture of nutrients, but many are particularly rich in one kind.

Energy foods

Your body uses energy all the time. Running, walking, and activities that involve moving around use up more energy than quieter activities, such as thinking, eating, and breathing. But even sleeping uses up energy. Most of your energy comes from the carbohydrates and fats that you eat. Carbohydrates include potatoes, rice, and food made from wheat, such as bread and pasta. Natural sugar is also a carbohydrate, so fruits like bananas and apples that contain natural sugars also give you energy.

Fats

Fats come from animals and from plants. Butter, whole milk, and cheese contain quite a lot of animal fat, while margarine and oils are fats that come from plants. The body stores any extra fat you eat as a layer of fat under the skin and within the body.

You Are What You Eat
Your body is made of the same kind of nutrients that you eat. Muscles are mainly protein, while your bones contain the minerals calcium and phosphorus. Under your skin is a layer of fat that helps to keep you warm.

This family is enjoying a meal that is rich in nutrients. Although we say they are enjoying spaghetti with meat sauce, they are really eating carbohydrates with protein and vitamin sauce!

Protein

Much of your body is made of protein. So as old cells wear out and die, the body needs constant supplies of new protein to build new cells. While you are still growing, your body needs extra protein to make millions of extra cells. Meat, fish, milk, and beans are all good sources of protein.

Vitamins and minerals

Most foods contain small amounts of vitamins and minerals. Minerals include zinc, calcium, iron, and phosphorus. Fruits and vegetables contain several vitamins and minerals. Milk and cheese contain different vitamins and minerals. Your body only needs small amounts of these chemicals, so as long as you eat a wide variety of foods in adequate amounts, you will get all the vitamins and minerals you need.

Water and Fiber

We usually think of healthy food as food that contains plenty of **nutrients.** But this book looks at two necessary ingredients that are not nutrients—water and fiber. They are not nutrients because they do not supply **energy,** help the growth of new **cells,** or contain **vitamins** and **minerals** that the cells need to function. Yet water is necessary for us to live, and fiber is necessary for a healthy digestive system.

Water

About two-thirds of your body is water. Bodily fluids such as blood, urine, digestive juices, and **mucus** are all mainly water. But all cells contain water, so even the parts of the body that look solid, such as muscles, skin, and other **organs,** contain water.

Body Fact
If you weigh 70 pounds (32 kilograms), about 46 pounds (21 kilograms) of that weight is water. This means that your body contains about 22 quarts (21 liters) of water.

Losing water

Your body is losing water all the time, mainly through urine and sweat. You need to take in clean water to replace the water that is lost every day. If you do not drink enough, your body begins to dry out. A person can live for several weeks without food, but after a few days without water, your body would become **dehydrated** and you would die.

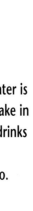

Drinking plain water is the best way to take in water, but most drinks and many foods contain water, too.

Fiber

Fiber comes from plants. It consists mainly of the hard walls of plant cells. At one time, people thought that fiber was simply waste that the body could do without. Later, scientists realized that fiber is needed to keep the digestive system healthy and working well. Fiber helps the body get rid of **feces** more quickly.

The digestive system

The digestive system breaks up food into pieces that are small enough for the nutrients in the food to pass into the blood. Most digestion takes place in the **small intestine.** Any food that is not digested passes through the **large intestine** and collects at the end of the intestine. It is passed out of the body through the anus when you use the toilet.

Getting rid of waste

Both water and fiber are important when it comes to getting rid of waste. It is easier to pass feces out of your body if the feces are moist and soft. Fiber absorbs water and so makes the feces bulkier and softer.

Eating an orange is a good way of taking in fiber and liquid. The drops of orange juice are held together by a thin film called a membrane. The membrane is fiber that is not digested.

What Is Water?

Water is made from two **elements**—**hydrogen** and **oxygen**—combined together. Both of these elements are normally gases, but when they combine together they form a liquid. Many substances **dissolve** easily in water, so water usually contains other chemicals, too. Some of these chemicals are **minerals** that your body can use. In polluted water, there are harmful **bacteria** that could harm your body.

Calcium in water

Some water contains a lot of calcium. Calcium is a mineral that makes your bones and teeth strong. Calcium makes the water "hard," and leaves a hard, chalky-white deposit on faucets and in pipes. It takes more soap to work up a lather in hard water.

Bacteria in water

Bacteria, like all forms of life, need water to live and breed. Typhoid, cholera, and dysentery are three serious illnesses that are caused by bacteria that live in water. These diseases are not common in the United States, but they kill thousands of people every year in parts of the world that do not have a clean supply of drinking water. The water you drink is treated to kill bacteria, which makes it safe to drink.

Tap water

The water from your faucet has been treated. The **sediment** is removed from the water. Then, chlorine is added to kill bacteria. In some places the mineral fluoride is added, too. Fluoride can help protect your teeth from tooth decay. It is added to most toothpastes.

Water is treated to make it safe to drink before it is piped to your home.

Water filters

Some people do not like the taste of tap water. Tap water is tested to make sure that it does not contain too many chemicals. Even so, many families use water filters. Some people think that water filters make tap water taste better.

Bottled water

Some companies bottle water that has been collected from underground springs. Many people think that bottled water tastes better than tap water. It does not contain chlorine or other chemicals that are added to tap water. But bottled water is expensive, and many people consider it an unnecessary luxury.

This pitcher contains a water filter. It is used to filter tap water of chemicals that can harm your body.

Water Fact
The water you drink is the same water that the dinosaurs drank! The earth's water is constantly **recycled**. It **evaporates** from the oceans and falls as rain. Some of the rain runs into lakes, wells, and underground springs. The rest flows into rivers and back to the oceans.

Water in Food

Even solid foods contain a lot of water. This is because all food comes from plants, **fungi,** or animals. Like all living things, they consist mainly of water. Some foods contain more water than others. Leafy vegetables, such as lettuce and spinach, have the most. They are more than 90 percent water.

Plants

Plants take in water from the soil through their roots. **Dissolved** in the water are **nutrients** that the plants need to stay healthy. The water and nutrients travel through narrow tubes up the stem to the leaves. Here, some of the water combines with **carbon dioxide** from the air to make food, using the **energy** of sunlight. The food is carried to all other parts of the plant—the flowers, fruit, stem, leaves, and roots.

Fruit juice

Fruit contains seeds that can grow into new plants. Some plants surround the seeds with sweet, juicy flesh. This kind of fruit contains a lot of water and is often made into fruit juice. The fruit of apples, oranges, grapefruits, pineapples, and grapes, for example, are squashed and the juice is collected and sold in bottles or cartons.

Vegetable or Fruit?
Although we think of cucumbers, eggplants, peppers, and tomatoes as vegetables, they are really fruits. Like other fruits, they have seeds inside them.

You can squeeze oranges to make orange juice. When the squeezing has finished, the only solids left will be the skin, the membranes, and the seeds.

Other food from plants

Nuts, grains, peas, and beans are seeds, too. They contain water, but not as much as juicy fruits. Most vegetables come from other parts of the plant and they are all rich in water. Cabbage and lettuce are leaves and contain the most water. Broccoli and cauliflower are flowers, while celery and asparagus are stems. Some plants store food in their roots. Potatoes and onions are two examples of root vegetables. Some vegetables, such as carrots, are juiced and sold as drinks.

Food from animals

Meat and fish are more than half water, but meat contains much less water than fruits and vegetables. Female cows, sheep, and goats make milk that we can drink or make into cheese or yogurt. Milk is about 90 percent water, so when you have a glass of milk, you are drinking mainly water. The other ten percent consists of **fat**, sugar, **protein**, **vitamins**, and **minerals.**

Dried food

Sometimes food is dried to preserve it. Raisins are dried grapes. Even so, these foods still contain some water. Dried dates, for example, are fifteen percent water.

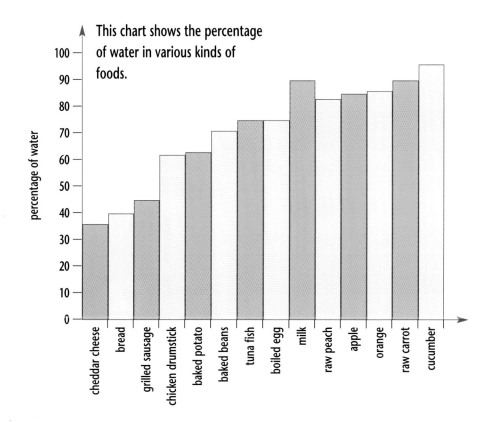

This chart shows the percentage of water in various kinds of foods.

What Is Fiber?

Fiber is a substance found only in plants, such as fruits, vegetables, and grains. The part of plant fiber that you eat is called dietary fiber. There are two kinds of dietary fiber—**insoluble fiber** and **soluble fiber.** Soluble fiber forms a gel when mixed with liquid. Insoluble fiber does not. Insoluble fiber also passes through your digestive system largely unchanged. Both types of fiber are important for a healthful diet.

Insoluble fiber

Most insoluble fiber is **cellulose,** a strong, rubbery material that forms the walls of all the **cells** that make up a plant. Leaves, stems, flowers, fruits, and roots all contain cellulose. Plant cells are too small to see, so you can usually not see all the fiber in a plant. However, some plants, such as celery and rhubarb, contain hard or stringy parts that are easy to see. Seeds, particularly beans and grains, are often protected with a tough outer skin that is rich in cellulose. The skin of an apple or a potato, for example, contains more insoluble fiber than the inside.

Digesting cellulose

Cellulose is a **carbohydrate** that cows, sheep, and other grazing animals can digest. Humans, however, cannot digest cellulose because the human digestive system does not contain the **enzymes** that are needed to break it down. So, although fiber is mainly made of carbohydrates, eating it does not give you any **energy.**

In this photo, you can see the stringy fibers that give these beans their strength. The tough skin that covers broad beans (also shown in the photo) contains cellulose, too.

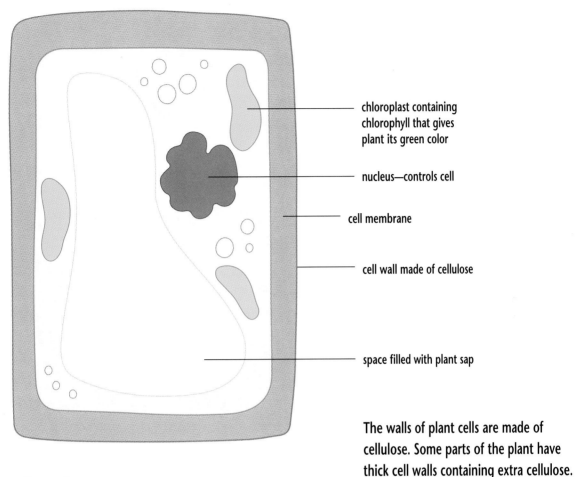

chloroplast containing chlorophyll that gives plant its green color

nucleus—controls cell

cell membrane

cell wall made of cellulose

space filled with plant sap

The walls of plant cells are made of cellulose. Some parts of the plant have thick cell walls containing extra cellulose.

Chewing

Because cellulose is so tough, it is difficult to chew. It takes longer, for example, to chew up a mouthful of raw carrot than it does to chew a piece of chocolate. And after chewing, you have more to swallow. Chewing helps your digestive system because it breaks up the food into smaller pieces before you swallow it. This makes it easier to digest. Also, the more you chew, the more **saliva** your mouth makes. Saliva contains an enzyme that starts to digest carbohydrates.

Soluble fiber

Soluble fiber includes pectins found in fruits such as apples and vegetables such as turnips and sweet potatoes. Pectins are carbohydrate substances found in the cell walls and **tissues** of certain plants. Soluble fiber is also present in oats. Soluble fiber in the diet can help to reduce the amount of cholesterol in the blood. It can also lower the risk of heart disease. Cholesterol is a waxy substance found in blood that helps form products the body needs. However, cholesterol can build up and narrow blood vessels.

Fiber in Food

Although you can clearly see stringy parts in many vegetables, the foods that are richest in fiber are nuts, dried fruit, beans, lentils, and peas. Grains, such as rice and wheat, also contain fiber. Rice and wheat, however, are often processed so that most of the fiber is taken out of them. This process is known as refining.

Nuts and dried fruit

Nuts are the seeds of some trees. They include pecans, hazelnuts, walnuts, and almonds. Nuts are rich in fiber, **protein,** and vegetable oil, which is a kind of **fat.** Dried fruits include dates, prunes (dried plums), and raisins (dried grapes). Apricots and cranberries are also often eaten dried.

Legumes

Legumes are seeds from pods, such as beans, lentils, and peas, and are rich in protein as well as in fiber. They are also low in fat. Peanuts are not actually nuts. They are legumes, but they have more fat than most legumes. Legumes are often used in soups. The Indian food dal is made from lentils mixed with spices, and the dip hummus is made mainly from chickpeas.

These foods are all rich in fiber.

In many countries, grains are ground by hand. This means that all of the grain is used and the flour is full of **nutrients** and fiber.

Grains

Grains come from crops such as wheat, rice, oats, corn, and barley. Breakfast cereals are made from grains. Wheat is ground into flour that is used to make bread, pasta, cookies, and cakes. Rice is normally eaten as a grain with meat or vegetables. How much fiber we get from grains depends on how much of the grain is used in the food. Brown rice and whole grain foods use all of the grain and so contain more fiber than white rice and refined flour.

Whole grain and refined foods

Whole wheat flour is ground from whole grains of wheat and is made into whole wheat bread, whole wheat pasta, and whole wheat crackers. White flour, most pasta, and white bread are made from wheat from which much of the fiber has been removed. All breads and pasta, however, contain some fiber.

Food with no fiber

Many foods contain almost no fiber. Milk and other dairy products, meat, and fish contain no natural fiber. Many other foods, such as chocolate, soda pop, and most cookies, have had all or almost all the fiber taken out.

Brown Bread and Fiber

Most whole grain breads are brown, but not all brown breads have a lot of fiber. You have to look at labels to see how much fiber the bread contains.

What Happens in the Digestive System?

The job of the digestive system is to break up the **nutrients** in food into pieces that are small enough to pass through the walls of the intestine and into the bloodstream. **Carbohydrates, fats,** and **proteins** are broken down into **molecules.** Water molecules are so small that they pass easily into the blood, but with **insoluble fiber** the opposite is true. It cannot be broken down enough, and so it is not absorbed and passes right through the digestive system.

In the mouth

Digestion begins in the mouth. The teeth slice, chop, and grind the food into smaller pieces that mix with **saliva** to make a soft mush. Chewing is particularly important in breaking up fiber. It makes the fiber soft and easy to swallow. When the mouthful of food has been chewed enough, your tongue pushes it to the back of your mouth and you automatically swallow it.

In the stomach

The mushy pulp passes down your throat, through the **pharynx,** and into the **esophagus,** the tube that joins your mouth to your stomach. The walls of the stomach make a strong **acid,** called hydrochloric acid. This acid usually kills off any germs in the food and starts to break the proteins up into separate molecules. Your stomach is a stretchy bag that stores and churns food for a few hours. The mushy pulp gradually changes into a kind of thick soup, called **chyme.** Every so often, some of the chyme squirts from your stomach into the **small intestine.**

Body Fact

In adults, the length of the digestive tube from the mouth to the anus is about 31 feet (9.5 meters) long. In children it is shorter. Multiply your height by 5.5 to get a rough idea of the length of your digestive tube.

In the small intestine

The small intestine is a long, thin tube. As chyme passes into the tube, it mixes with digestive juices that come from the **liver**, the **pancreas**, and the walls of the small intestine. **Enzymes** in the digestive juices get to work on the food, breaking up the carbohydrates, proteins, and fats. Gradually, these nutrients pass through the walls of the small intestine into the blood. Whatever remains, mainly fiber, digestive juices, and water, passes from the small intestine into a wider tube called the **large intestine.**

The digestive system breaks up foods. It changes the food from a bite-sized chunk of, for example, a peanut butter sandwich into a mushy pulp and then into a soupy liquid.

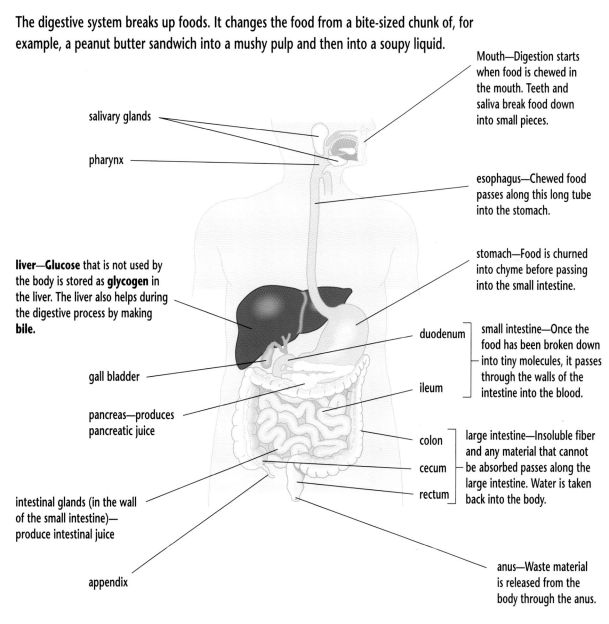

salivary glands

pharynx

liver—Glucose that is not used by the body is stored as **glycogen** in the liver. The liver also helps during the digestive process by making **bile.**

gall bladder

pancreas—produces pancreatic juice

intestinal glands (in the wall of the small intestine)— produce intestinal juice

appendix

Mouth—Digestion starts when food is chewed in the mouth. Teeth and saliva break food down into small pieces.

esophagus—Chewed food passes along this long tube into the stomach.

stomach—Food is churned into chyme before passing into the small intestine.

duodenum

ileum

small intestine—Once the food has been broken down into tiny molecules, it passes through the walls of the intestine into the blood.

colon

cecum

rectum

large intestine—Insoluble fiber and any material that cannot be absorbed passes along the large intestine. Water is taken back into the body.

anus—Waste material is released from the body through the anus.

Water, Fiber, and Digestion

Water passes easily through the walls of the digestive system into the blood. Some of it is absorbed in the stomach, but more is absorbed in the **small intestine.** The rest combines with fiber to form a mushy paste that passes into the **large intestine.** Here, more water is absorbed through the walls of the tube, and the paste gradually becomes more solid.

Fiber in the small intestine

Carbohydrates are broken up in the mouth, in the stomach, and in the small intestine. Fiber, however, is not able to be digested. It is absorbed in the small intestine and then passes largely unchanged into the large intestine.

Fiber in the large intestine

The undigested fiber travels slowly through the large intestine and forms one of the main parts of **feces.** Feces also contain digestive juices, **mucus,** dead **cells** from the walls of the digestive system, and **bacteria** from the large intestine.

The walls of the small intestine are lined with tiny fingerlike extensions called villi. They give the small intestine a bigger area for absorbing nutrients.

Harsh surroundings

The digestive system is a harsh place. The **enzymes** and **acid** in the juices that break down food so well can also attack the living cells of the digestive system itself. The walls of the stomach and intestines are protected by mucus. But even so, the lining of the stomach and intestines have a rapid turnover of cells. The cells only last a few days. As the cells die, they join undigested waste on its way through the system.

Water

As water is absorbed through the lining of the stomach and intestines, it can carry **vitamins** and **minerals** with it. More water is absorbed in the large intestine. As long as the body is not short of water, enough remains in the large intestine to make the feces soft and moist.

Getting rid of feces

Of all the food you eat, only a small fraction completes the whole journey through the digestive system. Feces are stored at the end of the large intestine. The feces travel from here into the rectum and are then passed from the body through the anus. A tight muscle in the anus relaxes to allow the feces to pass through.

This highly magnified image shows the mucus lining of the large intestine. The mucus helps the feces move and protects the intestine wall from damage.

Travel Time

Most undigested food takes about ten hours to reach the large intestine. It may take up to another twenty hours before it finally leaves the body.

Using Fiber

Most fiber is **insoluble fiber.** It is not digested and passes through the intestines with all the other waste matter. Fiber makes **feces** more bulky. Bulky feces help the **large intestine**, also sometimes called the colon, work better and help keep it healthy. The other kind of fiber, **soluble fiber,** can help prevent heart disease.

A long and winding journey

The **small intestine** is coiled within the folds of the large intestine. Food has to make its way through all the coils into the large intestine. Undigested food and waste then have to travel upward (against gravity), along and down to reach the anus, the final exit. The process by which food and waste are moved through the digestive tubes is known as peristalsis.

Peristalsis

The walls of the intestines contain circular bands of muscles. When a band of muscle contracts, or shortens, it pushes the food forward. At the same time, the band of muscle in front of the food relaxes, allowing the food to slide through it. The movement of each muscle relaxing and then contracting passes along the tube like a wave. The muscles in the small intestine work continually, churning the food around the tube, but the muscles in the large intestine work much more slowly.

Peristalsis Fact
Peristalsis moves food through the digestive system no matter what position your body is in. This means that even if you are upside down, you can still digest food.

Healthy colon

Fiber makes the waste bulkier and this gives the muscles of the intestines more to push against. They therefore work more often and more effectively. If you eat plenty of fiber and drink plenty of water, you are likely to pass feces about once a day. This keeps the muscles of the large intestine healthy, and it keeps **bacteria** and old waste from building up inside the colon. Some people pass feces more often and some people less often than once a day. What matters most is that the waste material is bulky and easy to push out of the body.

Absorbing cholesterol

Oats and foods such as apples and pears contain soluble fiber. Soluble fiber binds to **acids** released into the small intestine to help digest fats. The acids bound to soluble fiber cannot be reabsorbed for further use. Instead, they pass into the large intestine and form part of the feces. As a result, more cholesterol in the blood is converted into new acids. This is how soluble fiber in the diet helps lower blood cholesterol levels.

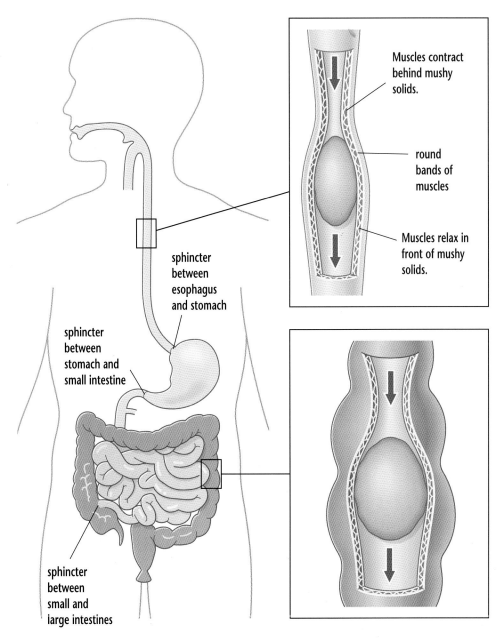

Muscles contract behind mushy solids.

round bands of muscles

Muscles relax in front of mushy solids.

sphincter between esophagus and stomach

sphincter between stomach and small intestine

sphincter between small and large intestines

Food moves through all the tubes in the digestive system in much the same way as you squeeze toothpaste out of a tube. Sphincters, which are muscles that contract, separate one stage of the digestion system from the next. They allow food to travel in only one direction.

Water in the Body

Water is the main ingredient of all the different fluids in the body, including digestive juices, blood, sweat, and urine. Each of these liquids needs water to make them runny. In addition, all the **organs** and **tissues** inside your body are coated with moisture. Salty water inside and outside the **cells** allows **nutrients** and chemicals to enter and leave each cell. Water is also involved in many of the **chemical reactions** that take place inside the body.

Digestive juices

Digestive juices, produced in the **liver** and **pancreas**, trickle through narrow tubes and into the **small intestine.** They join other digestive juices made in the mouth, stomach, and in the walls of the intestines.

Hitching a ride

Minerals, such as salt, and some **vitamins** can only be taken into the body along with water. They **dissolve** in water and pass with it into the blood. **Soluble fiber** also dissolves in water and is taken into the bloodstream.

Blood

The clear, watery part of blood is called plasma. This clear liquid has sugar and other nutrients dissolved in it. Red blood cells take in **oxygen** in the lungs. As the blood circulates around the body, every living cell is provided with a constant supply of food and oxygen.

Drinking plenty of water helps keep your skin moist and healthy. It also helps all the cells in your body work better.

Water in the cells

Water plays an important role in helping nutrients and oxygen pass from the blood into each cell. Chemical reactions inside the cells change **glucose** and oxygen into **energy,** while other reactions allow the cell to carry out its own particular tasks. Many of these chemical reactions involve water. Water then helps **carbon dioxide** and waste chemicals pass from the cell into the blood to be taken away and passed out of the body.

Urine and sweat

Waste chemicals are carried away from the cells by the blood and out of the body in urine or sweat. Urine is made in the kidneys. Sweat is made in the sweat glands and is pumped out of the body through tiny openings in the skin. Although you are only aware of sweating when you are very hot or the air is very moist, you are actually sweating all the time. Sweat is mainly water with salt and other waste chemicals dissolved in it.

Some parts of the body contain more water than other parts. This chart shows the percentage of water in different parts of the body. Surprisingly, the water content of the brain is higher than that of blood.

Water Fact
Your body produces 10.5 quarts (10 liters) of digestive juices every day. Most of this is water that is reabsorbed into the body.

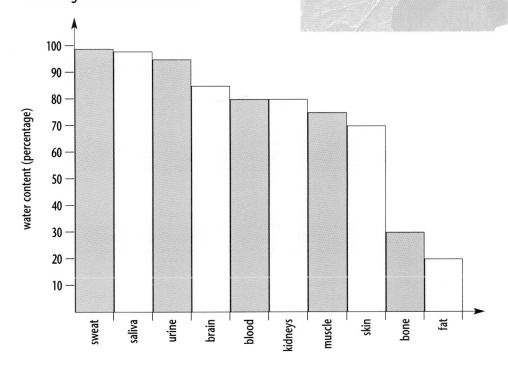

Water Balance

Your body loses water all the time. It loses water just from when you breathe, but it loses most water in the form of urine and sweat. Altogether, you probably lose about 3.2 quarts (3 liters) of water a day. To replace the water lost, you take in new supplies of water every day in your food and by drinking. Your body has to balance the water lost with the water taken in.

Urine

Nearly half of all the water you lose is urine. How much urine your kidneys make depends on how much liquid you have consumed and how hot the weather is. The more you drink, the more urine you make. However, when you are hot, you lose more water as sweat. To keep the amount of water in your body balanced, your kidneys then produce less urine.

Sweating

Your body loses water through the skin all the time, but when you are hot, you sweat much more. Sweating helps cool your body down. The water seeps out to your skin, but the heat of your body makes it **evaporate.** As it evaporates, it takes heat from your blood.

Breathing out

When blood reaches your lungs, **carbon dioxide** and water **vapor** pass from the blood into the lungs. These two gases then leave the body with the air that you breathe out. Every day, you breathe out the equivalent of 17 ounces (500 milliliters) of water in the form of vapor.

If you breathe out onto a mirror, the mirror will mist up with water droplets. These droplets have **condensed** from the water vapor in the air that you have just breathed out.

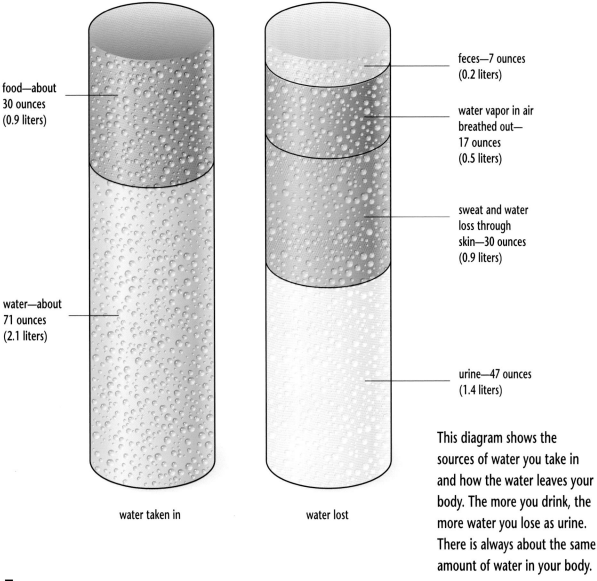

food—about
30 ounces
(0.9 liters)

water—about
71 ounces
(2.1 liters)

feces—7 ounces
(0.2 liters)

water vapor in air
breathed out—
17 ounces
(0.5 liters)

sweat and water
loss through
skin—30 ounces
(0.9 liters)

urine—47 ounces
(1.4 liters)

water taken in

water lost

This diagram shows the sources of water you take in and how the water leaves your body. The more you drink, the more water you lose as urine. There is always about the same amount of water in your body.

Feces

Feces contain water as well as fiber and waste materials. The water in feces makes it soft and easier to push out of the body. Usually only about six percent of water lost is in feces. But if you have **diarrhea,** a lot of extra water and salts may be lost. If you are suffering from diarrhea, it is important to drink extra water to make up for what is lost.

Thirst

Thirst is a strong signal that your body needs more water to balance the water lost. You feel thirsty when your mouth becomes drier because it is making less **saliva.** By the time this happens, your body is really short of water. You should drink regularly throughout the day, so that your body does not have to send you this emergency signal.

Water in the Kidneys

You have two kidneys, one on each side of the body just above your waist. They filter the blood and remove poisonous waste, such as **urea**, and extra water and salt. The water with salt and urea **dissolved** in it trickles from the kidneys down to the bladder where it is stored.

Poisonous waste

The main ingredient of urea is **nitrogen**. The **liver** changes the body's waste nitrogen into urea, a solid that **dissolves** easily in the water in the blood. The liver also breaks down other poisons in the body and turns them into harmless waste chemicals. These include chemicals that you would not usually think of as poisons, for example, the caffeine in cola.

In the kidneys

Each kidney is made up of over a million tiny filters. As blood enters a filter, water and everything dissolved in it is forced out of the blood. Most of the water and all the dissolved food and **nutrients** pass through the filter and back into the blood. What is left over is extra water with urea, salt, and waste chemicals dissolved in it. This is urine, and it trickles down one of the tubes called ureters into the bladder.

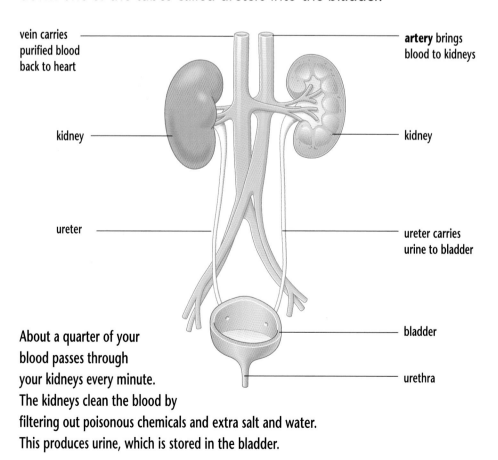

vein carries purified blood back to heart

artery brings blood to kidneys

kidney

kidney

ureter

ureter carries urine to bladder

bladder

urethra

About a quarter of your blood passes through your kidneys every minute. The kidneys clean the blood by filtering out poisonous chemicals and extra salt and water. This produces urine, which is stored in the bladder.

Extra water

You may think that drinking extra water will make your kidneys work harder, but in fact extra water makes it easier for your kidneys. The more water there is in your blood, the more diluted the extra salt and other wastes become. This means that each filter has to deal with less.

Urine

The kidneys send a constant trickle of urine into the bladder where it is stored. As the bladder fills up with urine, it stretches. Nerves in the walls of the bladder tell your brain when you need to urinate. If you wait until your bladder is very full, you will be very uncomfortable. The more liquid you drink, the more often you need to urinate.

Urinating

A ring of muscle at the bottom of the bladder usually keeps the bladder tightly closed. When you urinate, this muscle relaxes and urine flows out of your body from the bladder through a tube called the urethra.

Babies cannot recognize when they need to urinate. They cannot control the muscle that allows urine to leave the bladder. They wear diapers to absorb urine instead.

Bladder Fact

Your bladder can hold only about 17 ounces (0.5 liters) of urine at a time, but your body makes about three times this amount every day. This means that you have to urinate several times a day.

Too Little Water

If you do not drink enough water, you become **dehydrated.** This makes it difficult for your body to get rid of the poisonous waste chemicals in your blood. If you do not drink enough water for many hours, you will become thirstier and thirstier. People can survive for only a few days without water.

Dehydration

You do not always feel symptoms of mild dehydration, but as you become more dehydrated, you begin to feel thirsty. If you do not drink, you can begin to feel tired and dizzy. Dehydration can also cause headaches and a dry mouth.

Sweating

Sweating also causes dehydration, so you should always drink more liquid in hot weather or when you are in a hot place. Athletes and other people who exercise a lot can lose up to 1.8 quarts (1.7 liters) of sweat an hour and may be in danger of dehydration.

Severe dehydration

When people suffer from severe dehydration, all the

Tennis players often have to play hard in very hot weather. Players sip water in the breaks between games so they will not become dehydrated.

tissues in their body become short of water and cannot work properly. Their heart starts to beat very fast and their **blood pressure** falls. If they do not get treatment, they will go into **shock** and die.

Dying of thirst

When you think of people dying of thirst, you probably think of people stranded at sea or lost in the desert. But millions of people worldwide die of dehydration every year. Most of these deaths are due to dysentery, a disease that causes very bad **diarrhea.** Other people die of dehydration when they lose a lot of blood or suffer burns that cover a large area of their body.

Got Water?

One result of not drinking enough water is dry skin. You could also possibly have headaches and feel tired. These problems could be caused by dehydration. If you experience any of these problems, you might want to try carrying a bottle of water with you to drink during the day. Drink lots of water at home, too. You might notice that you have more energy, that your skin is not dry, and that you don't have headaches that often.

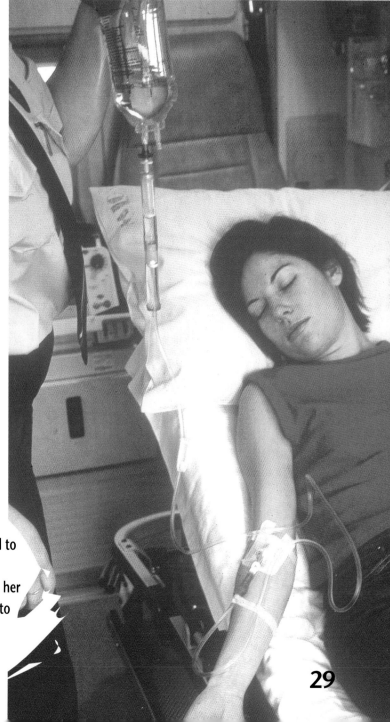

This girl has lost a lot of blood in an accident. Doctors decided to pump extra fluid—a mixture of water, **glucose**, and salts—into her veins. The fluid goes directly into her blood to keep her from becoming dehydrated.

Too Much Water

In normal circumstances, it is quite difficult to drink too much water. When you have consumed about one quart of water, your stomach will be full and you will not want to drink anymore. The people who are most likely to drink too much water are those who are trying to avoid **dehydration.** When a person becomes overheated, he or she may drink far too much liquid. Too much water upsets the balance of water and salt in the body and, in very rare cases, can cause death.

Balancing water and salt

Salt controls how much water passes out of the blood into your **tissues** to keep them moist. Your kidneys normally make sure that your blood contains the right amount of salt and water. But if the blood contains too much water and not enough salt, water leaves the blood and floods the tissues of the body.

Overheating

Athletes are one group of people who are at risk of overheating. People who take the illegal drug ecstasy are also in danger of overheating. Ecstasy can raise body temperatures above normal and cause extreme thirst. When you become hot, your body sweats to cool you down. Sweat includes salt and water, so your body loses both when you sweat. Sweating usually keeps your temperature about the same, but sometimes people become so hot that sweating cannot cool them. Highly trained athletes should know how much water they need to drink to prevent overheating. But the drug ecstasy makes people think that everything is great, even when things are going dangerously wrong.

Drinking water usually helps your kidneys work better. But if your kidneys cannot deal with the water, extra water may flood your body.

Flooded with water

Several ecstasy users have died from drinking too much water when they were overheated. Ecstasy users are in danger of becoming dehydrated. But, if they drink glass after glass of water, the amount of salt in the body becomes too watered-down. The drug ecstasy also keeps the kidneys from working correctly. Instead of the extra water being removed from the blood, it floods the tissues. The brain can become dangerously swollen. As it swells, it is squashed by the skull that protects it. Pressure on the brain quickly leads to **coma** and death.

Safe amount to drink

Athletes, and anyone who exercises a lot or is likely to become very hot, should drink about 17 ounces (0.5 liter) of liquid an hour. Sipping water or soft drinks will replace the water lost. Sports drinks are the best things to sip, since they include salts.

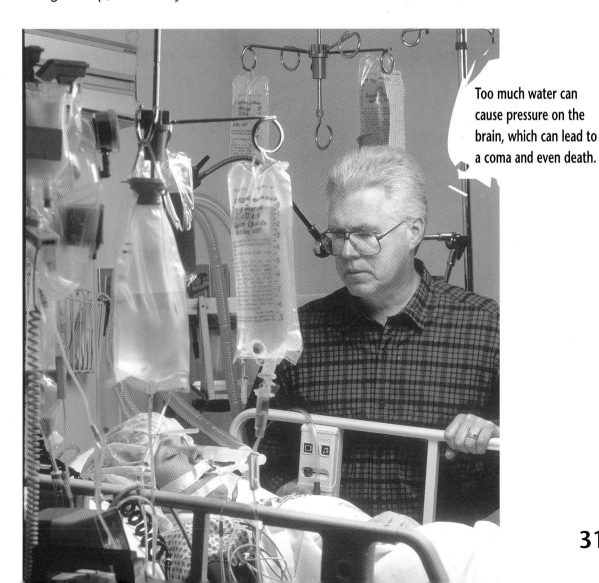

Too much water can cause pressure on the brain, which can lead to a coma and even death.

Too Little Fiber

If you do not eat enough fiber, your **large intestine** will work slowly and sluggishly. This may lead to constipation, which is difficulty in passing **feces.** Over a long period of time, constipation can lead to **hemorrhoids** and possibly cancer of the large intestine.

Moving along

Fiber and undigested food passes into the colon. Undigested food only moves through the colon when the muscles of the tube tighten behind it and push it forward. The less undigested food there is in the large intestine, the less often the muscles contract. This means that the undigested food stays in the colon for much longer than it should.

These foods contain almost no fiber. Only the tomato and the bun contain a little fiber. If you like to eat food like this, you should also include foods that are high in fiber, such as whole grain bread, fruits, and vegetables.

Constipation

How easy it is to push feces out of the body depends on how much fiber and water they contain. The longer the mushy paste stays in the colon, the more water from it is absorbed back into the body. This means that the waste material becomes dry and hard, which makes it difficult and painful to push it out of the body.

Testing transit time

Transit time is the time it takes for undigested food to pass through your body. It should be between 12 and 24 hours. One way to test your transit time is to eat a lot of beets. They will dye your feces red. See how long it takes for the undigested beet to pass out of your body.

Hemorrhoids

Constipation is unpleasant and can lead to future health problems. Adults who often suffer from constipation may develop hemorrhoids. Hemorrhoids are a condition in which the blood vessels in the anus and rectum become stretched and swollen. Hemorrhoids can be itchy and painful, particularly when passing feces.

Eating meals that contain plenty of fiber keeps the large intestine healthy and working well.

Colon cancer

Someone who has suffered from constipation for many years may develop colon cancer. People who live in North America, Europe, and Australia are more likely to get colon cancer than people who live in Africa and Asia. This may be because most Africans and Asians have a lot more fiber in their diets.

Too Much Fiber

Fiber in your diet makes your digestive system work smoothly. Eating more fiber than you are used to can cause extra gas to build up and maybe even **diarrhea.** Too much fiber can also keep you from getting enough **nutrients** if the fiber fills your stomach and keeps you from eating more nutritious food. Some fiber actually prevents certain **minerals** from being absorbed into the blood.

Gas in the large intestine

Adults normally have about about 6.76 ounces (200 milliliters) of gases in the digestive system. Children have a bit less. These gases come from various sources. Some of them are produced in the **large intestine.** There, billions of **bacteria** produce **methane, carbon dioxide,** and **hydrogen** as they feed on the undigested food. These gases have a bad smell and may pass out of you when you use the toilet.

Indigestion

Fiber is difficult to digest, so if you eat a lot of it, you may get indigestion. More undigested food in the large intestine gives the bacteria there more to feed on and so they produce more gas. Some foods, such as beans, cabbage, cauliflower, onions, and garlic, cause more gas than others. The extra gases fill the intestines, making your **abdomen** sore and swollen. Chewing your food for longer helps to prevent indigestion and reduces extra gas.

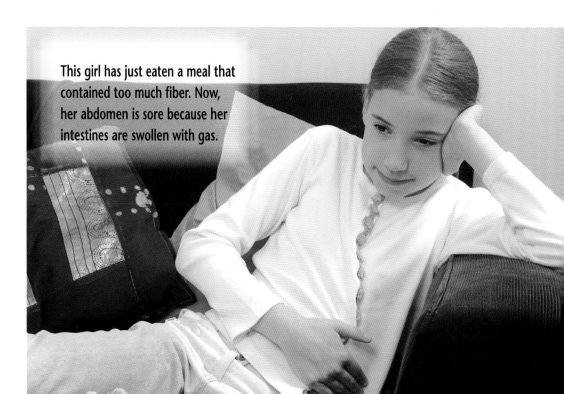

This girl has just eaten a meal that contained too much fiber. Now, her abdomen is sore because her intestines are swollen with gas.

Intestines can become irritated and cause discomfort if the wrong amount of fiber is eaten.

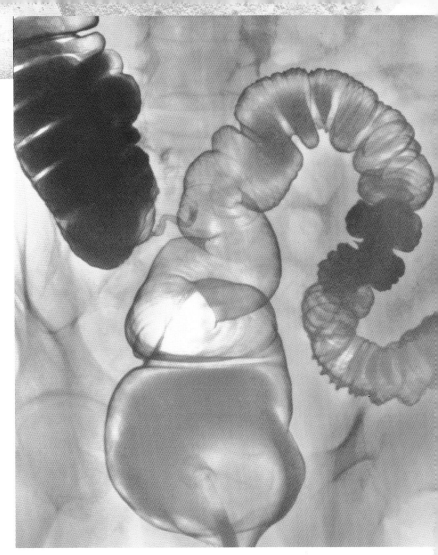

Diarrhea

Too much fiber can make your intestines irritated. In addition to causing pain, food is pushed through the intestines too quickly, so there is not enough time for the water to be absorbed through the wall of the large intestine into the blood. Extra water in the **feces** makes it very loose and runny, producing diarrhea.

Replacing nutrients

Young children especially should not eat too much fiber because it might replace nutritious food. It fills their stomach so that they stop eating before they have taken in enough **carbohydrates, fats, proteins,** and other nutrients.

Minerals

The fiber contained in the outer skins, or bran, of grains prevents some minerals, such as calcium, iron, and zinc, from being absorbed into the blood. Children in particular should not eat a lot of raw bran.

Gas in the Stomach

Most of the gas in your stomach comes from air that you swallow with your food and **carbon dioxide** from soda. If there is too much gas in your stomach, you usually burp to get rid of some of it.

Healthy Eating

In addition to getting the right amount of fiber, it is important to eat a good balance of **nutrients—carbohydrates, proteins, fats, vitamins, and minerals.** The Food Guide Pyramid provides information about a balanced diet. It divides food into six main groups, with suggestions about how much you should eat from each group each day.

Bread, cereal, rice, and pasta

These foods are rich in carbohydrates and so they give you **energy.** You should eat more servings from this group than from any other group—six to eleven servings. If you choose foods such as whole grain bread and brown rice, you will get lots of fiber, too. Granola, oatmeal, and bran cereals also contain good amounts of fiber.

Vegetables

Vegetables are rich in vitamins, minerals, and fiber. You should eat three to five servings of vegetables every day. All types of vegetables count toward the amount of servings.

Fruits

Fruits, like vegetables, are an excellent source of vitamins, minerals, and fiber. You should eat two to four servings from this group. Many fruits are good sources of both **soluble fiber** and **insoluble fiber.** The skin of an apple, for example, contains insoluble fiber and the inside of the apple contains soluble fiber.

Meat, poultry, fish, dry beans, eggs, and nuts

All these foods are rich in protein. Dry beans and nuts, however, are the only foods in this group that contain fiber. But protein is very important, especially for children who are still growing. You should eat two to three servings from this group every day.

Milk, yogurt, and cheese

These foods are rich in protein, vitamins, and minerals, particularly calcium. They do not contain any fiber. But they are nutritious foods, and it is suggested you eat two to three servings from this group each day.

Fats, oils, and sweets

At the top of the pyramid are fats, oils, and sweets. We should eat these "sparingly," that is, not often and in small amounts. These foods contain few nutrients and not much fiber. They are also high in fats and can lead to weight gain and health problems.

Tips for Healthy Eating
- Eat a wide variety of foods.
- Pay attention to serving sizes.
- Avoid eating too many fats, oils, and sweets

The Food Guide Pyramid shown below was created to give you an idea of what to eat each day to maintain a healthful diet.

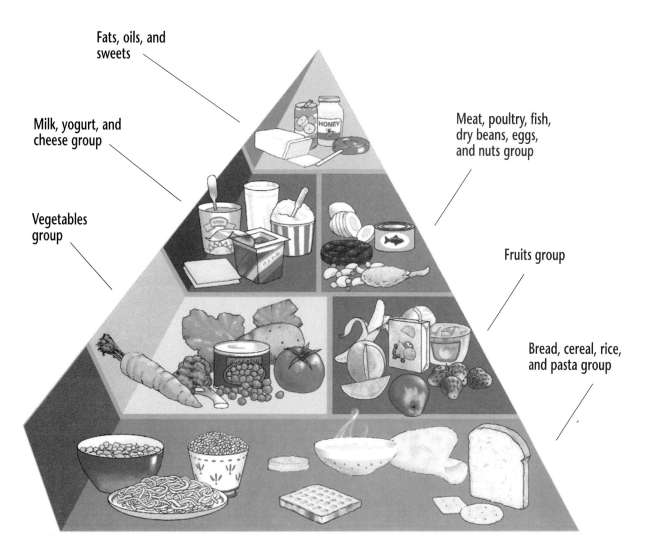

Fats, oils, and sweets

Milk, yogurt, and cheese group

Vegetables group

Meat, poultry, fish, dry beans, eggs, and nuts group

Fruits group

Bread, cereal, rice, and pasta group

Healthy Drinking

Your body loses up to about 3 quarts (2.84 liters) of liquid a day, mostly in the form of urine and sweat. You need to take in enough water to replace the amount lost. Your body gets nearly a third of the water it needs from food, but the rest must come from drinks. This means that most people should drink about 64 ounces (1.89 liters) a day.

Water in food

You will absorb water from the fruits and vegetables you eat every day, as well as from some of the other foods you eat. All food has some water in it, otherwise it would be too dry to eat.

This girl is enjoying a slice of watermelon. It contains a lot of juice and will help to replace some of the water she loses during the day.

Water in drinks

Soup and all types of drinks are mainly water. You can replace the liquid your body loses every day by drinking orange juice and other fruit juices, lemonade, and milk. But it is especially helpful to your body if you drink lots of plain water.

Caffeine

Cola, tea, and coffee all contain a substance called caffeine. Caffeine speeds up the processes in the body and makes you feel more alert. It also makes your kidneys produce more urine, so they remove more water from your blood. Most people can tolerate a certain amount of caffeine without becoming dehydrated. However, when you consume more caffeine than you are used to, it can cause mild dehydration.

Alcohol

Alcoholic drinks, such as beer and wine, are even more dehydrating than caffeine drinks. People who have consumed a lot of alcohol often suffer from something called a hangover afterward. A dry mouth, tiredness, sick feelings, and headaches are common symptoms of a hangover. Most of these symptoms are caused by dehydration.

The bottle of water shows you how much you should drink every day. The glasses show one way of drinking this amount of liquid.

Healthy Diets

Your diet consists of all the foods you usually eat. Many people in North America, Europe, and Australia eat a diet that is too low in fiber. People from other parts of the world eat food that usually contains much more fiber. Vegetarians and vegans follow special diets, but these diets usually contain plenty of fiber.

Traditional diets

Most people in the United States use wheat flour, but people in Africa, Asia, and South America often make flour from other grains, such as corn and rice. Their diets often include beans, peas, or lentils, which are rich in **nutrients** and fiber. Traditional recipes from these areas are now quite popular in other parts of the world, including the United States, as people realize how healthy and tasty they are.

Vegetarian and vegan diets

Vegetarians do not eat meat or fish. Vegans do not eat any food that has come from animals, such as dairy products or eggs. Vegetarian diets may be healthier than meat diets, because they are usually high in fiber and low in fat. Vegan diets are also usually rich in fiber, but vegans have to choose their food carefully to get all the nutrients they need.

These children are enjoying couscous, a dish from northern Africa. It includes chickpeas and meat in a spicy sauce and is served with semolina, a grain food that is rich in fiber.

Watch What You Eat

A lot of people like burgers, fries, and chocolate. But these foods can make some people overweight. If a doctor recommends that you need to lose some weight, you can try eating whole wheat bread and spaghetti instead of fatty foods. The fiber in the food will keep you from feeling hungry. Drink plenty of water as well. This will also help to make you feel full. Healthy snacks to eat are bananas, apples, and raw carrots.

People who are ill

People who are ill often do not feel like eating very much at all. It is, however, very important that they do not stop drinking water. If you are throwing up or suffering from **diarrhea**, you need to drink plenty of water to replace the water lost. Also, if you have a high temperature, or fever, you need to drink plenty of extra water to replace all the water lost through sweating.

When you have a high temperature or a sore throat, you may not feel like eating very much, but it is very important that you drink plenty of water.

Daily Needs

Most Americans eat about 0.25–0.35 ounces (7–10 grams) of fiber a day, but nutrition experts recommend that adults get 0.88–1.06 ounces (25–30 grams) a day. Children should have less fiber, depending on how many **calories** they eat per day. An adult that eats about 2,000 calories a day needs 0.88 ounces (25 grams) of fiber. But children eat fewer calories than

This meal contains 0.26 ounces (7.3 grams) of fiber and 10 ounces (289 milliliters) of water.

adults. If you consume 1,200–1,300 each day, then you will need only about 0.53–0.63 ounces (15–18 grams) of fiber. Young children should have much less fiber. Also, while adults should drink about 64 ounces (1.89 liters) of liquid a day, you do not need to drink quite as much.

Food		Amount containing about 0.35 ounces (10 grams) of fiber
Fruit	Apples	3 apples
	Bananas	5 bananas
	Oranges	5 oranges
Vegetables	Broccoli	3 stalks
	Carrots	3 carrots
Legumes	Baked beans	2 cups
	Lentils	2 cups
	Peas	2 cups
Grains	White bread	15 slices
	Whole wheat bread	5 slices
	Oat bran cereal	1 cup
	All-bran cereal	1/2 cup

Amount of fiber and water in different foods

Food	Amount of fiber in 3.5 ounces (100 grams)	Amount of water in 3.5 ounces (100 grams)
Apples, including skin	0.06 oz (1.7 g)	2.9 oz (85 ml)
Baked potatoes	0.10 oz (2.7 g)	2.1 oz (63 ml)
Bananas	0.12 oz (3.4 g)	2.5 oz (75 ml)
Beets	0.07 oz (1.9 g)	2.8 oz (82 ml)
Cooked brown rice	0.03 oz (0.8 g)	2.2 oz (66 ml)
Cooked spaghetti	0.04 oz (1 g)	2.5 oz (75 ml)
Cornflakes	0.03 oz (0.8 g)	0.1 oz (3 ml)
Cucumber	0.02 oz (0.6 g)	3.2 oz (96 ml)
Oranges	0.06 oz (1.7 g)	2.9 oz (85 ml)
Peaches	0.06 oz (1.7 g)	3.0 oz (89 ml)
Peanut butter	0.19 oz (5.4 g)	0.03 oz (1 ml)
Peas	0.17 oz (4.7 g)	2.6 oz (78 ml)
Raw mushrooms	0.04 oz (1 g)	3.1 oz (93 ml)
Raw tomatoes	0.04 oz (1 g)	3.1 oz (93 ml)
Sweet corn	0.05 oz (1.5 g)	2.4 oz (72 ml)
White bread	0.05 oz (1.5 g)	1.3 oz (38 ml)
Whole wheat bread	0.20 oz (5.8 g)	1.3 oz (38 ml)

ounces = oz	grams = g	milliliters = ml

Glossary

abdomen part of the body that contains the stomach and small intestine

acid chemical compound that aids in digestion

amino acid smaller unit or building block of proteins. Different amino acids combine together to form a protein.

artery tube that carries blood from the heart to different parts of the body

bacteria microscopic living things. Some are helpful, like those in our intestines, but some can cause disease.

bile substance made in the liver that breaks up the fats in food

blood pressure pressure the blood puts on the walls of the blood vessels as it is pumped around the body

calorie measurement of energy supplied by food

carbohydrate substance in food that the body uses to provide energy. Foods rich in carbohydrates include bread, rice, potatoes, and sugar.

carbon dioxide one of the gases in the air. Animals breathe out carbon dioxide.

cell smallest unit of a plant or animal

cellulose substance that the walls of plants cells are made of

chemical reaction when two or more chemicals react together to produce a change

chyme mushy liquid that passes from the stomach to the small intestine

coma state of deep sleep from which a person cannot wake up

condensed the condition when a gas or a vapor, such as water vapor, cools and changes into a liquid

dehydrate decrease the amount of water in something

diarrhea condition in which the feces are loose and watery

dissolve break down or mix with a liquid so that the liquid is the same throughout

element simple substance made up of only one kind of chemical

energy ability to do work or to make something happen

enzyme substance that helps a chemical reaction take place faster

esophagus tube through which food travels from the mouth to the stomach

evaporate when a solid or a liquid becomes a gas

fat substance found in a wide range of foods. The body can change fat into energy. Fat is stored by the body in a layer below the skin.

feces undigested food, bacteria, digestive juices, and dead cells that are passed out of the body as solid waste

fungus simple living thing such as a mushroom, yeast, or mold

glucose simple form of sugar that is broken down from carbohydrate food during digestion

glycogen substance made from glucose that is stored in the liver and muscles following absorption

hemorrhoids swollen veins around the rectum, often caused by a diet low in fiber

hydrogen invisible gas that is one of the gases in the air. Hydrogen combines with other substances to form, for example, water, sugar, proteins, and fats.

insoluble fiber type of fiber that cannot be broken down by the human digestive system, such as the bran in whole wheat bread.

large intestine part of the intestines through which undigested food passes after it has left the small intestine

legume type of food that includes lentils, peas, and beans. Legumes are the seeds of some plants and are rich in protein.

liver organ in the body that plays a role in digestion. It makes bile and helps clean the blood. People also eat beef and chicken livers, which are a rich source of vitamins and minerals.

methane gas that occurs naturally in the earth and is made in the body in the large intestine

mineral nutrient found in foods that the body needs to stay healthy

molecule smallest unit of a substance that is still that same substance and still has the properties of that substance

mucus slimy liquid made in the body

neutralize to make something neutral, that is, neither acid or alkaline

nitrogen invisible gas that is the main gas in the air. Nitrogen is one of the elements that make up amino acids.

nutrient substance found in foods that helps the body grow and stay healthy. Carbohydrates, proteins, fats, vitamins, and minerals are all nutrients.

organ body part that has a particular job to do. An eye is an example of an organ.

oxygen   gas present in the air and used by the body. Oxygen is one of the most common elements and is used by the body to make amino acids.

pancreas   gland that produces various digestive juices that flow through a tube into the small intestine

pharynx   back of the throat

protein   complex chemical that the body needs to grow and repair cells

recycled   reused, sometimes in another form

saliva   watery liquid made by glands in the mouth and the inside of the cheeks

sediment   solid particles that collect at the bottom of a container of liquid

shock   condition caused by a drop in blood pressure that can cause a person to pass out

small intestine   part of the intestine into which food passes from the stomach to be digested and absorbed into the blood. Undigested food passes right through the small intestine into the large intestine.

soluble fiber   fiber that dissolves in water and passes into the blood

tissue   material made up of cells that forms a part of an animal or of a plant

urea   substance formed from waste material in the liver

vapor   gas that rises from a liquid or solid

vitamin   nutrient needed by the body in small amounts

Further Reading

Ballard, Carol. *The Digestive System.* Chicago: Heinemann Library, 2002.

Brownlie, Ali. *Why Are People Vegetarian?* Austin, Tex.: Raintree Publishers, 2002.

Connolly, Sean. *Ecstasy.* Chicago: Heinemann Library, 2000.

D'Amico, Joan, and Karen Eich Drummond. *The Healthy Body Cookbook.* Hoboken, N.J.: Wiley & Sons, 1999.

Hardie, Jackie. *Blood and Circulation.* Chicago: Heinemann Library, 1998.

Kalbacken, Joan. *The Food Pyramid.* Danbury, Conn.: Children's Press. 1998.

Royston, Angela. *Eating and Digestion.* Chicago: Heinemann Library, 1998.

Stille Darlene R. *The Digestive System.* Danbury, Conn.: Scholastic Library, 1998.

Toriello, James. *The Stomach: Learning How We Digest.* New York: Rosen Publishing, 2001.

Westcott, Patsy. *Diet and Nutrition,* Austin, Tex.: Raintree Publishers, 2000.

Index

alcohol 39
amino acids 4

bacteria 8, 18, 20, 34
bladder 26, 27
blood 6, 22, 26, 30
bones 4
breathing out 24

caffeine 26, 39
calcium 8, 35
cancer 33
carbohydrates 4, 12, 16, 18, 35, 36
carbon dioxide 10, 23, 24, 34
cells 4, 5, 6, 18, 19, 22
cellulose 12–13
chewing food 13, 16, 34
cholesterol 13, 21
constipation 32, 33

dehydration 6, 28–29, 30, 31, 39
diarrhea 25, 29, 34, 35, 41
digestive juices 17, 18, 19, 22, 23
digestive system 7, 16–19, 20, 21, 22, 34
dried fruit 11, 14

ecstasy 30–31
energy 4, 10, 12, 23, 36
enzymes 12, 17, 19

fats 4, 11, 16, 21, 35, 36, 37

feces 7, 18, 19, 20, 25, 32, 33, 35
fiber 6–7, 12–15, 16, 18, 20–21, 22, 32–35, 36, 40, 41, 42, 43
    daily requirements 42
    insoluble fiber 12, 13, 20
    soluble fiber 12, 13, 18, 20, 21, 22
Food Guide Pyramid 36–37
fluoride 8
food groups 36–37
fruit and vegetables 10, 11, 12, 13, 14, 21, 36, 38, 42

gases 34, 35
grains 15, 36, 42

healthy diets 40–41
heart disease 13, 20, 21
hemorrhoids 32, 33

illness 4, 8, 41
indigestion 34

kidneys 24, 26–27, 30, 31, 39

large intestine (colon) 7, 17, 18, 19, 20, 32, 33, 34

legumes 14, 42

meat and fish 5, 11, 36
milk and dairy foods 4, 5, 11, 36, 40
mucus 6, 18, 19
muscles 4, 6, 20

nutrients 4–5, 10, 16, 19, 22, 23, 26, 34, 36, 40
nuts 11, 14

overheating 30–31
oxygen 22, 23

peristalsis 20
plants 10–11, 12, 13
proteins 4, 5, 11, 16, 35, 36

refined foods 14, 15, 40

saliva 13, 16, 25
salt 22, 23, 26, 27, 30, 31
seeds 11, 12, 14
small intestine 7, 16–17, 18, 20, 22
sweat 6, 23, 24, 25, 28, 30, 38, 41

thirst 25, 28, 29

urine 6, 22, 23, 24, 25, 26, 27, 38, 39

vegetarians and vegans 40
vitamins and minerals 4, 5, 8, 11, 19, 22, 34, 35, 36

waste chemicals 23, 26, 28
waste material 7, 18, 19, 20, 25, 33
water 6, 7, 8–11, 18, 19, 20, 22–31, 33, 35, 38–39, 41, 43
    bottled water 9
    loss 6, 24, 25
    tap water 8–9
    water balance 24–25, 30, 31
    water cycle 9
    water vapor 24, 25
water filters 9
whole grain products 15, 36